John Royston Pearson

Hints on the construction and management of

orchard-houses

John Royston Pearson

Hints on the construction and management of orchard-houses

ISBN/EAN: 9783337150273

Printed in Europe, USA, Canada, Australia, Japan

Cover: Foto ©Lupo / pixelio.de

More available books at **www.hansebooks.com**

INTERIOR VIEW OF THE LARGE ORCHARD-HOUSE AT THE
CHILWELL NURSERIES, NOTTINGHAM.

HINTS

ON THE

CONSTRUCTION AND MANAGEMENT

OF

ORCHARD-HOUSES.

By J. R. PEARSON,

THE NURSERIES, CHILWELL, NEAR NOTTINGHAM.

SECOND   EDITION.

LONDON:

JOURNAL OF HORTICULTURE AND COTTAGE
GARDENER OFFICE,

162, FLEET STREET, E.C.

1862.

LONDON:
PRINTED AT THE HORTICULTURAL PRESS,
17, JOHNSON'S COURT, FLEET STREET.

PREFACE

TO THE SECOND EDITION.

THE first edition of this little book was written under the conviction that erroneous ideas of the construction and management of orchard-houses were calculated to retard the spread of this delightful mode of cultivating fruit trees. An opinion appears to be prevalent, that any kind of a wooden shed covered with glass is an orchard-house, and that any or no management would have for its result the production of a good crop of fruit. Whilst travelling in Scotland I heard of houses, the sides of which, being made of half-inch boards, and these not closely joined, afforded such imperfect protection, that, in that severe climate, even the trees were killed during winter. Not only in Scotland, but in England, many of these structures have been erected in such a rough and imperfect manner, that they are inefficient for the purpose they were intended to serve, and are anything but an ornament to the gardens in which they are placed. Knowing that every failure was a fact eagerly welcomed by those who oppose everything new, I wished to show that before the system could be fairly tried, it was necessary to have a house adapted for the purpose, and a certain amount of information on the part of the person having the care of it. The gradual improvement which has taken place in building orchard-houses shows that these impressions were not without foundation. The success of my little book was as gratifying as it was unexpected.

CHILWELL, NEAR NOTTINGHAM,
August, 1862.

CONSTRUCTION AND MANAGEMENT

. ORCHARD-HOUSES.

SINCE these useful structures were first invented, a great number have been built in various parts of the country, and though many have answered admirably, I have been surprised to hear of some partial or entire failures. When our house was first erected, we had no man on the grounds who had ever grown a fruit tree in a pot; and yet we had a good crop of Peaches and Nectarines the first year. Indeed the whole culture appears so simple, that I have been quite surprised to learn of difficulty being experienced by a person capable of growing any plant in a pot. It is after all a little unreasonable to expect that every person

should find easy what appears simple to our-
selves. Anything is easy when it is known how
to do it. Few persons fail to grow a Geranium
or a Fuchsia in a tolerable manner, because their
first attempt was made amongst friends who knew
how to direct them. If they had to begin without assistance the culture of a plant which they
had never seen before, and had but little acquaintance with the growth of plants in general,
the chances of success would not be greatly in
their favour. Though Vines have been so long
cultivated in this country, and vineries are now
so common, how few persons grow good crops of
Grapes every year! yet those who know how, tell
us what is quite true, that nothing is so easy to
fruit as a Black Hamburgh Vine; and that if
planted in good soil, nothing but bad management can prevent its fruiting. When we think
that few persons know anything of the management of Peach trees, still less of their culture
under glass, it is not surprising that the first
time they attempt to grow them some want of
success should attend their efforts. No oral or
written instructions will make up for the lack of
practical knowledge, because it is impossible to

guard against or foresee every possible mistake. But yet I have thought a few plain directions, founded on our own experience, and intended to guard against the mistakes that I have seen committed, might be useful. Let us, then, commence by saying a few words as to the construction of an orchard-house.

HOW TO BUILD AN ORCHARD-HOUSE.

When the idea of growing fruit trees in glass houses occurred to Mr. Rivers, it was necessary for him to find some other plan of erecting them than in the costly mode greenhouses were generally built; and he therefore invented cheap wooden houses, which his own workmen erected. These, under his management, succeeded so well, that he wrote his interesting little book, "The Orchard-House," and recommended the same manner of construction to others. His statements of the very low price at which a house could be constructed, caused considerable excitement amongst the builders; and the natural result was, a conviction of the necessity of altering their plans and charges. A good house may be

built at a half or third of what it would have cost
some little time ago. The readers of " *The Cottage Gardener* " may recollect, that Mr. Rivers
stated his large house, covering about 2400 feet
square, cost £140, or 1s. 2d. per foot square of
ground covered. This house is built on oak posts
set in the ground, and is without raised beds,
paved walks, or indeed any description of brickwork whatever. I have just built a house of which
the frontispiece is a view of the interior.   The
figure at page 45 represents the exterior. It covers
2700 feet square, with 18 inches of brickwork
above the surface; the walks are paved with
black and buff quarries, the bricks laid in Port-
land cement, and the whole finished in a style fit
for *any* garden, at a cost of £230, or about 1s. 8d.
a square foot of ground covered.   It is therefore
unnecessary to have an ugly orchard-house to
obtain a cheap one, or one that depends on
wooden posts set in the ground for its stability.
An orchard-house should not be less than 20 feet,
nor more than 30 feet in width. No fire being
used to keep out frost, a wide house, containing
a large body of air, will cool more slowly than a
    rrow one; and plants blooming in a 20-feet

house would be safe from frost, when those in one 14 feet wide might be in danger.

If a house be more than 30 feet, it must have a ridge-and-furrow roof, which, though necessary when large spaces have to be covered, is more expensive and much heavier in appearance. To grow fruit of fine flavour, light is the great requisite; and that the sun should shine as equally as possible on both sides, it is desirable that your house be span-roofed, if possible, having one end towards the south. The Peach, like the Geranium, is attacked by the green smother fly or aphis; if you have to smoke a badly-constructed house, you will wish it better built, and in a very cold spring the advantages of close-shutting windows must be acknowledged. An orchard-house should be built so that it could be turned into a vinery, greenhouse, or hothouse, if at any time it might be desired to do so; and I have no hesitation in saying the span-roof is the best form for either the growth of Vines or plants. Vines, in a lean-to house of any height, require a ladder to prune or gather the fruit, and there is always a tendency to produce the finest foliage and fruit on the upper part of the rods; whilst, by being trained across a span-roof, the sap is checked, the growth rendered more equal, and both Vines and fruit are more within reach. Plants, in a lean-to house, invariably draw towards the light; whilst in a span-roofed house, they have the advantage of light on all sides.

It will be seen from the above remarks that I have no intention of showing in detail how an orchard-house ought to be built, mine are only " hints " as to their construction. Having had twelve houses erected within the last few years, each being an improvement on the former ones; and seeing that Mr. Foster who built them and · is largely engaged in their manufacture, is constantly making improvements in their construction, I have arrived at the conclusion that amateur building is a mistake. It appears advisable to take advantage of experience acquired at other people's expense rather than make mistakes at our own cost. The houses built by Mr. Foster, of Beeston, near Nottingham, are by far the best I have hitherto met with. They are constructed of all sizes, adapted to the requirements of the smallest or the largest establishments, and they are not only of an ornamental, but a durable character. The mode by which Mr. Foster ties the span of his houses, and renders them firm in their construction, is particularly meritorious, and far superior to anything I have yet seen for strength and elegance. It is perfectly novel in design, and has been secured by a patent. Exception has been taken to my strongly-expressed dislike of lean-to houses by several practical gardeners for whose judgment I have a high respect. It must be admitted they have advantages for very early forcing in some situations. A thick brick wall forming the north side of a vinery in a very cold and windy district will economise artificial heat, and sunk pathways in front, narrow passages, and low roofs will not much inconvenience a gardener in his shirt sleeves and cloth cap. A conservatory or orchard-house ought to be constructed, so that ladies may enjoy a walk in them with no more feeling of constraint than in an open garden; to be able to cut a flower, reach a Peach, or water a plant without difficulty, is essential to the enjoyment of such houses. It is not sufficient to be able to get inside, exclaim How beautiful! and wish to be out again as soon as possible. Similar objections may be urged against covering Peach walls with glass; a covered wall is no place for enjoyment.

The frontispiece is taken from a photograph of our large house 30 feet wide, of which *fig.* 1 is a

Fig. 1.

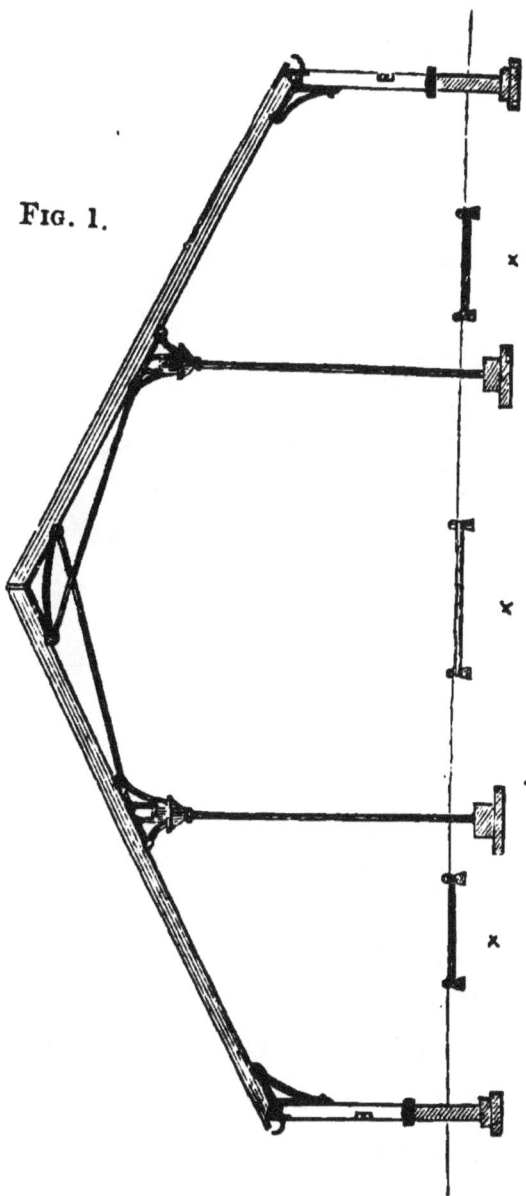

Section of House Erected by Mr. Foster, of Beeston.

section. There are three paved walks, bordered by round-headed tiles, which have a very neat appearance. The iron pillars rise out of the beds, and carry both purlin and rafter, as seen in *fig.* 2.

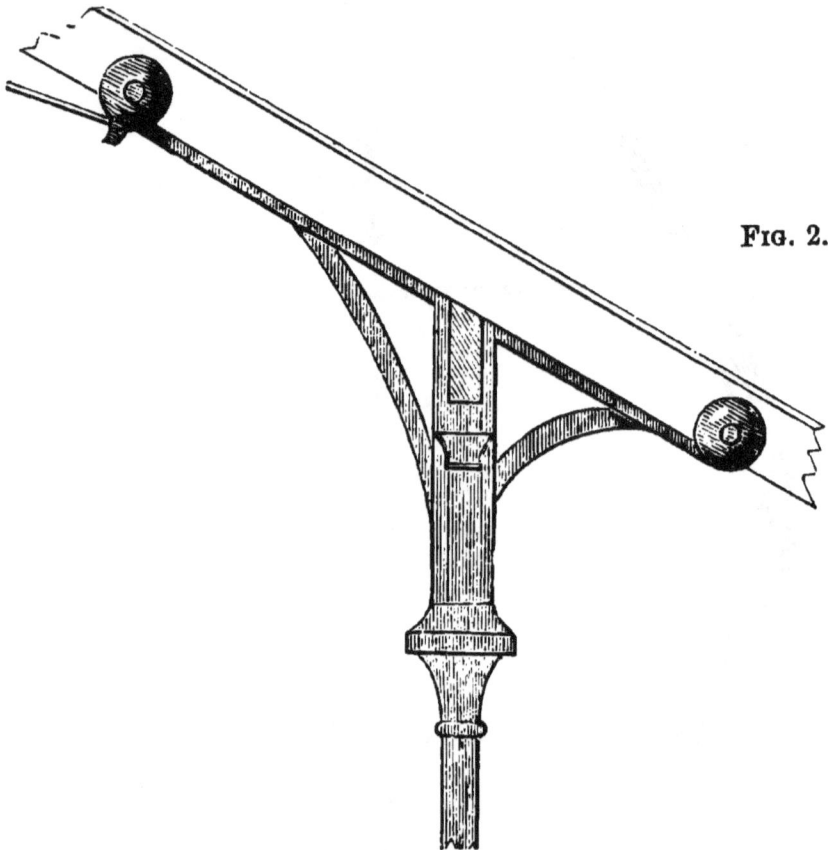

FIG. 2.

Head of Column carrying Purlin, and into which the End of Tie-rod is screwed.

The upper part is also tapped to receive one end of the tie-rod, which screws into it; the other extremity is represented in *fig.* 3.

Fig. 3.

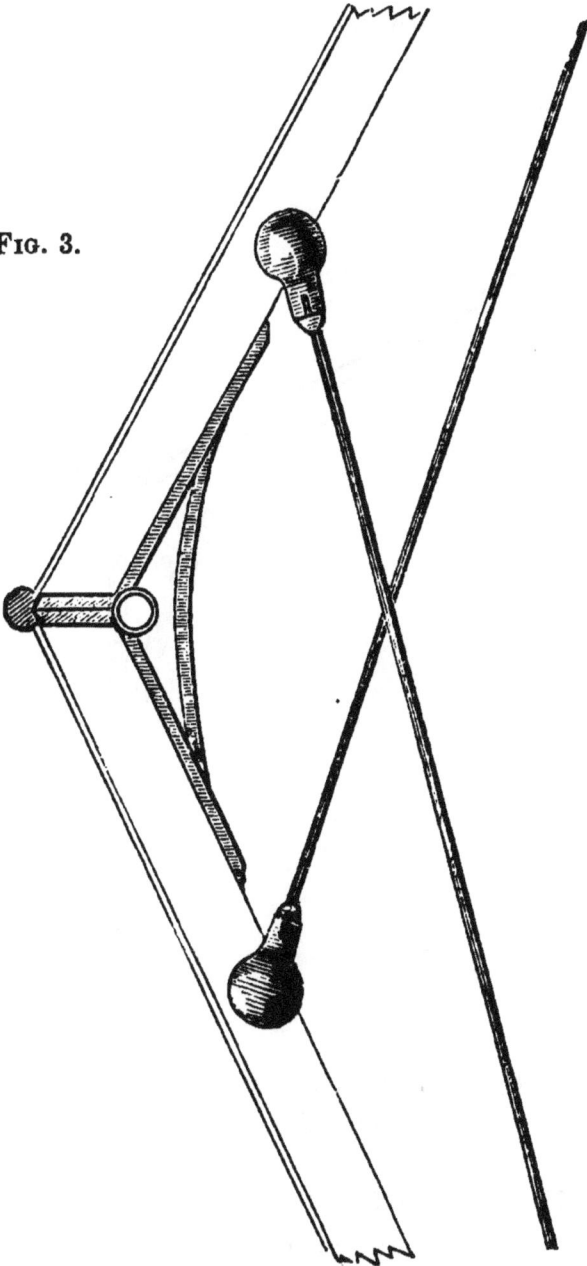

Part of Section, showing Cross Ties and Ridge Supports.

MOVEABLE HOUSES.

Having often heard the remark, "If I were

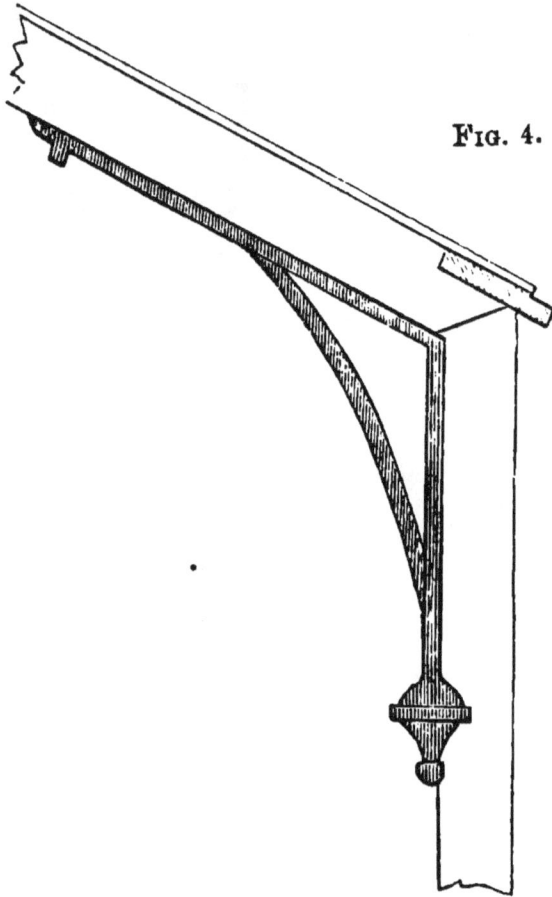

FIG. 4.

Bracket. In moveable houses this is part of the iron casting on which the house stands.

living on my own property I would have an orchard-house immediately," I have great pleasure

c

in calling attention to Foster's patent moveable
house on iron supports. It is as strong as any
house can be built, and yet may be taken in
pieces and removed without difficulty. *Fig.* 5 is
a section of one of these houses 14 feet wide, the

FIG. 5.

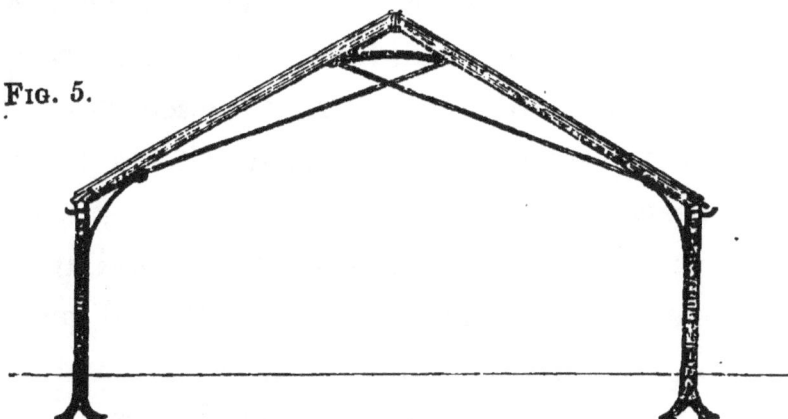

Section of House 14 feet wide.

path being in the centre. The feet, pillar, and
bracket are all cast in one piece. The roof is
made in separate lights, and also the ends and
sides, so that there is no occasion to break a pane
of glass in removing the whole structure. I have
just had a house erected on this principle, 60 feet
by 24 feet, heated by six rows of pipes. It is
intended for a conservatory, and is a beautiful
building; compared with Paxton's " Houses for
the Million " its advantages will be acknowledged.

Sir Joseph is probably not answerable for the illustration which appears in the gardening periodicals, in which a triangular greenhouse is so ingeniously filled with six trees, reminding us involuntarily of the three degrees of comparison. Supposing the trees figured to be Orange trees, what a pity the artist did not give us a representation of the gardener sponging the leaves of one of the outer plants, or clipping its shoots to prevent them touching the glass, which they are in great danger of doing. His position would appear less comfortable than that of the jolly old gentleman in the middle walk, who seems so contentedly viewing his *well-proportioned* trees.

However appropriate as vineries they must be most inconvenient for the growth of plants.

A friend has just sent me a pamphlet entitled "A Handbook of Vine and Fruit Culture, as adapted to Sir Joseph Paxton's Patent Hothouses, by Samuel Hereman." It contains some extraordinary designs of houses filled with "impossible-to-be-cultivated plants;" it pre-supposes an immense amount of ignorance and credulity on the part of the public, to give a section of a house formed of two eight-feet lights, placed at

an angle of 35°, and represent it as containing
seventeen rows of plants, as at page 9. At
page 10 the three degrees of comparison are re-
produced. At page 17, a house is figured, the back
wall of which 6 feet high is furnished with shelves
six in number, one above another like books in
a library—a most capital idea for a Chinese garden, and admirably adapted for liliputian trees.
Page 18 represents a most ingenious house, a
shelf overhead, 6 feet from the ground, four
shelves of plants on the back wall, and three rows
in the path, four rows on a front stage, and a
hanging-basket all in a house 7 feet wide; but the
chef d'œuvre of these very original designs will
be found at page 50, in which a lady, a fountain,
twelve birds, two Vines, two Peach trees, a hanging-basket filled with Ferns, and a plant in a pot,
all find accommodation in a house, which, from
the scale, appears 20 feet wide and 13 feet in
height. I cannot congratulate Sir Joseph Paxton
on his supposed connection with this remarkable
and very amusing publication.

Mr. Foster's houses on iron supports are really
as good and durable as those built of brick; the
effect of the crossed-iron rods is very superior to

the straight ones in the house figured in Mr. Rivers' new edition of " The Orchard-House," a section of which I reproduce. A house with a

Fig. 6.

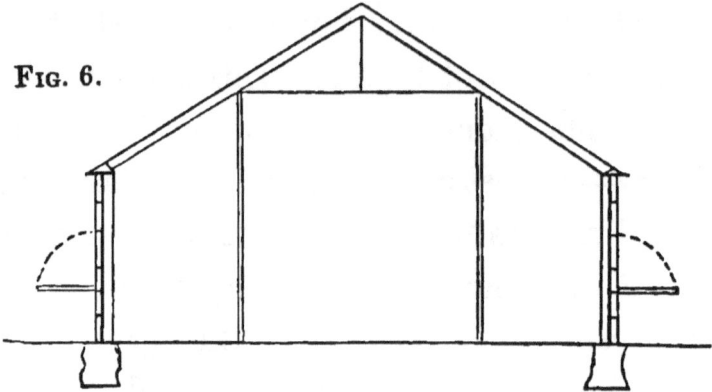

Section of Mr. Rivers' House.

number of parallel tie-rods has the appearance of a covered drying ground, and is suggestive of the laundry. Perhaps this idea occurred to the artist who made the section of Mr. Rivers' large house, page 25 of the last edition of his work, as the rods are there not represented.

MANAGEMENT OF AN ORCHARD-HOUSE.

After your house is built, if not before, you will have to determine the fruit to be grown in it. Tastes will differ, of course, but the Peach, Nectarine, and Apricot may be considered the

aristocracy of the orchard-house. Plums bear
enormous crops, but are not increased in flavour.
Pears are very handsome, but ours were so inferior in flavour, that we discarded them. Both
Plums and Pears might be grown in the house till
all danger from frost was over, and then turned
out to grow and ripen their fruit, which would
give more room to the Peaches and Apricots. I
will suppose Peaches only to be grown, and con-
fine my remarks to them, as the same management applies alike to Nectarines and Apricots.
Buy your plants, if possible, early in the autumn ;
you will not only have a better choice, but plants
potted late seldom set their fruit well the following season.

After the first year, if it is intended to pot or
only top-dress the trees, do it before the leaves are
quite off, or as soon after as possible. Choose a
good turfy loam (the top spit from a clay pasture
is the best), and add to it about a fourth of rotten
manure : this will be better if mixed some months
beforehand. Pot very firmly. If your soil be
· light, you can hardly make it too solid. Of course,
the soil must be moderately dry. No plant enjoys
tempered mud. A good rule by which to judge of

the state of soil is this : if a handful, grasped
firmly, retains its shape, but separates when
allowed to drop on the floor, it will not be too
dry or too wet. If Peaches are growing in borders, or against the walls, it is very necessary to
keep the ground firm about their roots; trample
the soil well when in a dry state, and if the soil be
light, use a rammer to make it solid. If in the
autumn any copper-coloured fly be seen feeding
on the Peach shoots, paint the trees infested with
¼ lb. of soft soap, ¼ lb. of sulphur, 2 quarts of
tobacco water, 2 quarts of soft water, and a little
clay to thicken the mixture, taking care not to
injure the buds during the operation. If the trees
are free from insects, and have not been infested
with red spider, no dressing will be required.
The mixture of Gishurst Compound, before recommended, has been found injurious. The cow-
manure usually employed to dress trees on walls
gives rise to a species of mildew in the orchard-
house, clay is preferable. When the plants have
been painted, place them closely together in the
middle of the house, and cover the pots well with
leaves, hay, or straw, to keep them safely from
hard frost. During frost the house had better be

closely shut, and open only in mild weather. If the soil in the pots be moist when covered with leaves in autumn, they will probably not require watering more than once or twice during the winter; if not dry as dust, the plants will be none the worse for having been kept without much water whilst destitute of leaves.

When the buds are swelling, prune the trees if they require it, and put them in the places which they are intended to occupy during summer. In pruning, care should be taken to cut to a wood-bud, otherwise all the fruit on a leafless branch will fall afterwards. However pruned, a few branches will be in this leafless state at the time of blooming; these may be at once cut back to where there are leaves. If the plants have been properly grown the previous year, they will re-quire little or no cutting. Stopping during sum-mer answers the same purpose as pruning in spring—that is, keeping the plant compact and of the shape preferred. Many persons think they must commence the culture of every fruit tree by pruning it, and because fresh-planted trees are often better for having a few of their branches shortened to counterbalance the mutilation of their

roots inevitable from transplantation, they think
the same treatment necessary for a tree established
in a pot, whose short, well-ripened shoots are full
of blossom-buds. The pruning of Peaches, in par-
ticular, had better be deferred till the plants are
almost in bloom, as it is very difficult to distinguish between wood and flower-buds earlier in the
season. It is generally supposed safe to cut to
triple buds; but some kinds have the habit of
producing triple flower-buds, so it is safer to
wait till they are easily recognised by their colour.

The later your plants bloom the better; the
house should, therefore, be well ventilated, and
kept cool till the plants are in bloom. From the
period the flowers are fairly out till the fruit is set
is the critical time of orchard-house management.
Let us suppose the house all in order, and the
plants coming into bloom, cultivate them as if they
were a number of Geraniums. If it is warm out of
doors—that is, if the wind is soft and mild—venti-
late freely; but do not, because the sun shines,
subject your trees to a cold east wind. It is often
safe to open the west side of the house when it is
advisable to keep the ventilators on the east side
closed. If there be any sign of smother-fly not a

day must be lost in getting rid of it, or you may give up all hopes of Peaches for one season. These pests increase so rapidly, and the Peach leaf is so tender and liable to curl, that great mischief is done before you are aware; and though you may recover the plants, the fruit is gone. Tobacco smoke will kill the green smother-fly, and so will tobacco water, but the latter must not be used whilst the plants are in bloom. If the copper-coloured aphis is seen, smoke at once; but do not trust to smoke; look the plants over, and if you see any insects alive, touch them with a small painter's brush that has been dipped in a mixture prepared in the following manner:—Boil ¼ lb. of quassia in a gallon of soft water for ten minutes, strain, and add to the water ¼ lb. of soft soap. No species of aphis can withstand this application.

I have lately heard a very high character of the tobacco paper prepared by Griffiths and Aviss, of Coventry. It is very cheap, and said to be far more efficacious than tobacco for fumigating. I have ordered a large quantity, and shall be happy to let any one have a little to try its effects.

Let me repeat: you must keep your plants free

from insects. Nothing is easier, if taken in time. Of course, this is not written for gardeners; they know that a man who has a house full of plants infested with insects, is no gardener, or an idle one, or so foolish as to undertake more than he can carry out, in which case he will in time lose both place and character for ability.

As strong tobacco smoke will sometimes prove injurious to Peach blooms, it is better to prevent the necessity of fumigation if possible till the fruit is set. If the plants are kept clean till they are in flower it may generally be avoided.

Next to allowing the Peach to be devoured by aphis, the non-fertilisation of the blooms is the greatest cause of failure. Most persons know that the farina or pollen of the stamens must come in contact with the pistil, if perfect fruit is to be produced. To this end Providence has placed honey in the nectaries of flowers, as an attraction to bees and other insects, which, in buzzing about, distribute the pollen.

A moment's consideration of this subject will explain the cause of many failures. Of course the farina cannot fly if not in a dry state; a damp atmosphere, therefore, tends to prevent the setting

of fruit. It will be an advantage to have your
plants in bloom, when there is a chance of the
weather being warm enough to allow of ventilation, and the assistance of bees, to fertilise the
flowers. The span-roofed house affording the
means of ventilation near the ground on both
sides, the whole length of the house is much
superior to the ugly glazed sheds, called lean-to
houses, generally built. If orchard-house trees
are in good health, and the weather be warm
when they are in bloom, and bees in abundance,
they will probably set three times the fruit they
can bring to perfection ; but as it is better to leave
nothing undone to insure success, we always fertilise the flowers by touching them with a camel-
hair pencil, in the middle of a warm sunny day.
It takes but a very short time to go over every
plant in a large house. It is the opinion of many
besides Mr. Darwin, that not only is the pollen of
some varieties of a species stronger than others,
but that when applied to a different plant or
variety, it is more efficacious. In using a perfectly
dry camel-hair pencil, it will be found, that though
the farina of each bloom may be distributed, but
little can be carried away by the brush. Let us,

then, take a lesson from Nature. Pull off a bloom and open it lengthwise, and it will be found sticky with honey in the inside; insert the brush, and it will then, when afterwards used, be soon covered with pollen, and you will thus cross variety with variety. If the petals soon begin to drop and leave the base of the flowers attached to the tree, you have been successful, and may hope for a crop. I have been thus explicit, because aware that this is a matter of importance, and often neglected.

A slight blow on the stem of a tree will produce the same effect, but with less certainty. In doing this use the hand only, for fear of injury to the bark, which might induce gumming.

How frequently, after a wet blooming season, have people been surprised that their Apple and Pear trees have such a poor crop of fruit! The trees were so full of bloom, and there was no frost; how could it be? It rained every day, and the farina could never leave the stamens. Or perhaps the Peach trees in the forcing-house are without fruit. No wonder; whilst they were in bloom the place was hot and damp, and no insects stirring. Let us suppose the fruit safe, the petals most of them fallen : a dry atmosphere will now be injurious. Syringe the trees with soft water early in the day, so that the leaves may not be wet when a hot sun shines on them. As the temperature increases, do the same about four o'clock, and shut the house up while warm. Why should you lose the advantage of the heat that the house has acquired, by giving air all night, as recommended by some persons? The plants will soon show you, by their appearance, that they, equally with the Vine, enjoy the still warm and damp atmosphere, and the red spider will have but little chance of thriving. If you put half a pint of tobacco water into a large watering-pan of soft water when syringing, say once a-week, it will be found a great *preventive* of insects, though it would not be strong enough to kill them if you had allowed their increase. If any leaves are perceived having a mottled appearance on their upper surface, there will probably be found red spider on the under side. If they cannot be seen with the naked eye, a lens will be an assistance. Syringe with plain water first to wet the foliage, and then syringe the under side of the leaves with 2 ozs. of Gishurst to a gallon of soft water, and

wash it off well the next morning.* In using
either Gishurst or soft soap, always take care that
it is well dissolved in the water, or it is sure to do
harm to leaves and young shoots, Gishurst being
a soap, it will not dissolve in hard water. I believe
a want of attention to this has caused injury,
where the quantity used has not been in excess.
When the fruit commences to ripen, all syringing
must be discontinued—an additional reason for
keeping the plants perfectly clean up to this period.

The plants being in a growing state, it will be
necessary to determine the shape they are to
assume. I prefer a conical form, some admire a
bush, and others a close-growing tree like a spike
of Hollyhock flowers. Whatever may be the
form determined upon, it is easily given by stopping all those branches which are growing too
fast, and leaving those only which are growing in
the desired direction. A branch may be stopped
when it has made but three or four leaves; it will
then, in all probability, recommence growing. If
so, after three or four leaves are formed stop it
again. This should not be repeated a third time, if

* Never use Gishurst Compound to growing plants of greater
strength than this—*i.e.*, 2 ozs. to the gallon of water.

it can be avoided, because the shoots often do not ripen enough to form good wood-buds : and the whole branch, though full of blossom, is lost the following season for want of leaves to draw up the sap.

The trees should not be allowed to carry too much fruit whilst young, or they will be weakened, and the fruit be inferior in size and quality. The first season twelve to fifteen will be quite enough to bring to perfection; but they must not be thinned to that number at once. As much fruit drops during the process of stoning, they should be thinned a second time when they are a little bigger than marbles. Till the middle of June, move the pots occasionally, to prevent the trees rooting into the border; after that time let them remain quiet till the fruit is ripe. A few root-lets in the soil below the pots will do good, but if these become too strong, it is no advantage to the fruit, and an injury to the tree when required to be moved. Some of my finest Peaches have been gathered from trees which have never rooted through the pots. When the fruit is the size of walnuts—say the middle of June, give them manure water once a-week—not drainings from a manure yard, or guano water, but made in the following manner:—Take a mixture of sheep, horse, and cow-manure, in equal parts, or any of them, if you cannot get all three, and put it into a trough or old tub; then cover it with scalding water, to kill all insects and their eggs; afterwards add water, and let it settle, using the supernatant liquor. When you add fresh water, stir it up from the bottom, and let it settle again. The value of these manures, if employed separately, is in the order I have placed them.

I have often used this compound in quite a thick state, and I think with advantage. Of course it leaves a deposit on the surface of the soil, roots form under it in large numbers, and it checks evaporation. If the surface becomes too compact and will not admit water, it is broken by stirring with a pointed stick.

Never give water until it is required, and then give enough to reach the bottom of the pot. A want of attention to this rule has probably caused the death of more plants than any other mismanagement.

In a well-constructed house, there is little, if

D

any, danger from frost; but in our changeable
climate, it is difficult to foresee what may happen.
In 1859, I think, a frost of very great severity
occurred whilst Peaches were in full bloom. The
house in which our fruiting plants were growing
(the first erected here) has wooden sides, and
spaces between the boards; one end is also of
wood. I now think it not only ugly, but a very
imperfect protection; yet we have never failed to
raise a crop in it every season. But the morning
after the frost alluded to occurred, no one, on
entering the house, would have given much for
the chances of a crop. The trees had a very
wretched appearance; but after being syringed
with cold water before sunrise (on the same principle that dictates rubbing a frozen nose with
snow), they were none the worse for what had
happened.

Having given these few plain directions for the
management of orchard-house trees, some opinion
may perhaps be expected as to the relative advantages of pot culture, and planting the trees in the
open borders of the house. I am trying both
plans, and at present give the preference to pots.
The Peach tree is so easily fed by manure water,

that the fruit from a tree in a pot is quite as large as that from one planted out. In a cold summer like that of 1860, the roots in pots were warmer than those in beds, even where raised above the surface of the surrounding land, and the fruit generally of a finer flavour. Trees in pots can be moved about, placed nearer or wider apart, and are less in the way when the house requires painting—in short, they are more conveniently managed on every occasion than when growing in a bed. Fruit trees always make wood enough, often too much, if their roots are unconfined, so that, except requiring less water, there appears no advantage in turning them out of pots.

In a dry warm house ants are often a great annoyance, eating the stamens and ovary out of Peach blossoms, and afterwards attacking the fruit. When trees are trained to a wall the ants will mount in spite of every precaution.

One of the advantages of cultivating Peaches in pots, is the facility of destroying ants' nests by hot water.

Many gardeners will be glad to know that if before the fruit is ripe a mixture of treacle and arsenic, be put on small pieces of glass and placed near their runs, it will be eagerly taken and soon lessen the number of these troublesome insects.

Another question has often been put to me, Will potted trees last—that is, continue in a healthy state? I have seen trees which have never been repotted, but only top-dressed for nine years, and which are as healthy as ever. My belief is, that the average life of orchard-house trees will be greater than those trained on open walls, subject as these latter are to so many injurious influences. The Orange has long been cultivated in pots and tubs, and trees are in existence, in perfect health, hundreds of years old, as all know who have visited Versailles. As an experiment, and to show what might be done with a Peach tree, I had a small plant of Royal George Peach potted in what is called a two-quart pot: it was not allowed to root through the bottom, and it was well fed by manure water; thirteen Peaches were ripened, and these were amongst the best fruit in the house. Early in the autumn, before it shed its leaves, it was taken up, all the earth shaken from its roots, and placed again in the same pot, and it has now seven fine Peaches on it. The plant has only three small shoots, is about 18 inches in height, and is in better health than last year.

In all cases, especially in reference to luxuries, the cost of production is a necessary or reasonable inquiry. In this respect there is no comparison, not only with fruit that requires forcing, but with wall fruit. A house 60 feet by 20 feet wide, costs about £100, and will produce, say 150 dozen a-year. This is a moderate calculation. There is no reason to expect failure in a well-managed house. How much wall would be required to give the same results with certainty? Then, in respect to flavour, in the average of seasons, there is no comparison between wall and orchard-house fruit. A Peach or Apricot which has only one side exposed to the sun, can never be evenly ripened, nor, consequently, of the highest flavour. How stupid it must be to perpetuate this in fruit-houses, as is often done with Peaches on a trellis. I have heard the observation, " Why, these are like Cape Peaches, not at all like English ones; they are so full of juice, and so much higher in flavour than any I have tasted in England: " the reason being that the sun had shone all round the tree, and the fruit had been protected by the foliage.

Some persons pull off the leaves from their Vines, to expose the Grapes to the sun; and instead of well-coloured fruit, get "*Red* Black Hamburghs," with thick skins.

There is a prevalent idea that an orchard-house ought to be heated to render it safe from frost, and to ripen the wood in autumn. I should be very sorry if this were generally thought necessary, having had good crops every year myself. I cannot, of course, advise any one to incur an outlay in the first instance equal to half the cost of the house, beside the after expense of fuel. Fires require much and constant attention, as all know who have had the care of them. The great enjoyment of an orchard-house is the agreeable temperature, the shelter from cold winds, and absence of damp artificial heat. If the wet and sunless summer of 1860, followed by the terrible winter of the same year, did not prevent our trees bearing a good crop of fine fruit, why should we fear for the future? To this reasoning may be added, that if you provide the means of heating your orchard-house, you afford a great temptation to your gardener to fill it with tender plants, which require a little heat to keep out frosts.

This will forward the blooming-season, and probably result in a loss of the fruit-crop. A Peach tree grown in a properly-constructed house *must* ripen its wood, unless very crowded or shaded by Vines. In this part of England fire is quite unnecessary to mature the wood of a Peach tree under glass, and certainly is injurious to the flavour of the fruit. A Peach, to be in perfection, should not be too ripe; one that falls from the tree, though unbruised, is never in first-rate condition. Some kinds, of which Crawford's Early is an instance, will hang till quite woolly. The experienced eye detects at a glance when a fruit ought to be gathered; to feel a Peach is to spoil it.

Amongst the many advantages afforded by the orchard-house, certainly not the least is the protection of the dormant fruit-buds during a severe winter. Many a gardener covers his trees with great care during spring, when all chance of a crop has perhaps been destroyed for months. After a very severe winter, on examination of a blossom-bud before it is expanded, it will be perceived that the pistil is dead or injured, and though the tree may be full of flower, of course

there will be little or no fruit.   But it is probable
that where there has been no apparent injury, the
embryo bloom may have suffered.   In the autumn
of 1859, I had six Apricot trees, which were all
cultivated alike, and potted at the same time; three
were placed in the orchard-house, and three on a
bed in the open garden, and the pots were covered
a foot thick with leaves.   The following spring
the latter were removed to the house, and they
bloomed as well as those which had been under
cover during winter; no difference could be perceived in the appearance of the flowers; but
whilst the fruit on the protected plants had to be
severely thinned, two of those which had been
left in the open garden were entirely without fruit,
and the third bore only four Apricots.

Now let me say a word to those gardeners who,
having learnt their business, are afraid to commence a culture they do not understand, or who
really do not believe in the orchard-house.   Whatever you may do or say, they will be built.   Gentlemen will not be satisfied to be without fruit, when
their neighbours have plenty; or to have two or
three kinds only, instead of a variety of sorts,
lasting over a long period, and varying in appear-

ance and quality. You will find it pleasanter, in cold spring weather, to be under glass, than nailing trees against a wall. For four or five months the orchard-house is no trouble. If walls already exist, they will be very convenient for choice Pears, and you will have a chance, by the same means, of furnishing Ribston Pippin Apples, White Calville, &c., fit to be eaten. In advertisements we shall soon see, " Wanted, a Gardener familiar with Orchard-house Culture." These structures, being without fire heat, are such agreeable places to walk in during cold east winds, and afford so much comfort to the aged and infirm, that they will be built, and young gardeners will do wisely to learn how to manage them.

To nurserymen I would say, though orchard-houses are a luxury to others, they are a necessity to you. None know better the difficulty experienced in procuring Peaches and Nectarines true to name, leaving out of the question those rogues who will purposely substitute one kind for another, how few have the means of fruiting all the varieties of Peaches and Nectarines on walls. Without specimen plants to furnish buds, how is it possible to keep a stock tolerably correct to name? Working from plants growing in the nursery, a mistake once made, will perhaps be perpetuated for years. If you buy a new variety, and have no means of proving it, you may propagate and sell large numbers of a perfectly worthless kind, or one quite unsuited to your climate. Without an orchard-house, it is impossible to compare leaf with leaf, blossom with blossom—the only way of gaining an intimate acquaintance with fruit trees. Whilst walking through a large nursery last summer, I was able to convince the foreman, who accompanied me, that the majority of his Peach and Nectarine trees were incorrect. His reply was, "Well, I am not to blame; Master buys largely, and I have to work from plants remaining unsold: we have no means of fruiting them."

HOW TO DISTINGUISH THE DIFFERENT VARIETIES OF PEACHES AND NECTARINES.

There is probably no tribe of fruit trees the varieties of which are so little known by cultivators in general as Peaches and Nectarines. The fruit of many kinds resemble each other so much in appearance, that they are difficult to distinguish when removed from the tree.

From the uncertainty of our climate, good fruit is rarely seen on open walls, perhaps not oftener than once in three years. So many trees in gentlemen's gardens are incorrectly named, that it is no matter of surprise few can distinguish a Peach with certainty. I was lately shown a number of Peach trees full of fruit by a nobleman's gardener, all named Royal George, and asked to account for their differing in quality so markedly, as they were all growing on the same wall. He would hardly believe me at first, when I told him there were in reality three kinds. By observing the leaves, blossom, and fruit, almost any variety may be named without difficulty.

Peaches and Nectarines are divided into two classes by their blooms, and into three by their leaves. The fruit may also be described as separating easily from the stone, or firmly adhering to it; the former are termed melting, the latter clingstone. The blossoms are large and handsome, or small and inconspicuous. The leaves are serrated on the edge, without glands (see *fig.* 1);

crenated with globose glands (see *fig.* 2); or crenated, with reniform glands (see *fig.* 3).

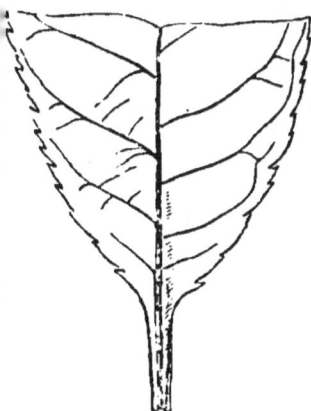  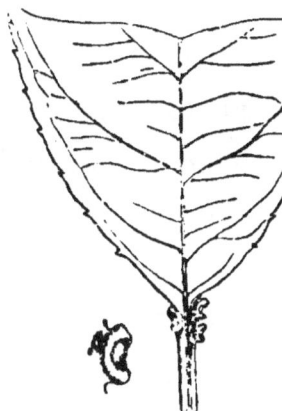

Fig. 1.   Fig. 2.   Fig. 3.

Now, let us see how these characters will enable
us to identify a variety. We will suppose you
have a fine melting dark-coloured Peach; it had
small red flowers, and you are told it is Royal
George; it has globose glands at the base of the
leaf near the foot-stalk, you may be almost certain
it is a Galande. You will not be able perhaps to
say if it be the French or English Galande, as
these two varieties resemble each other in all three
particulars—a very rare case; even when of the
same race, they will generally be found to differ
either in flowers or leaves. We will suppose, however, your fine dark melting Peach has globose
glands on the leaves; but had large handsome

blooms; it is Grosse Mignonne, in all probability. Thus you will be able generally to name a variety with certainty, and, at any rate, be in a position to detect mistakes. This information is the more necessary, as many unprincipled persons have been in the habit of substituting a variety easily propagated for one more difficult to cultivate, This accounts for the fact, that hundreds of persons who think they know the Grosse Mignonne Peach have, in all probability, never seen it.

The following Peaches and Nectarines are arranged according to our ideas of excellence, beginning with Grosse Mignonne, the finest of all orchard-house Peaches. If a list of kinds suitable to open-air cultivation in the midland counties were given, this fine variety would, in all probability, be omitted, and French Galande occupy the first place.

PEACHES.

In the second and third columns the letter G signifies *globose*; R, *reniform*; S, *serrated*. M, *mid-season*; E, *early*; L, *late*.

1 Grosse Mignonne, or Grimwood's Royal George	G	M	Fruit large, yellow and red, so tender as to mark with a touch; blooms large, dark pink, quite ornamental. There is an early variety of this almost equal to it in quality

2 Noblesse	S	M	Large; in the orchard-house yellowish-white, some varieties slightly striped pink. Sulhamstead is a vigorous seedling of this kind, differing but little from its parent; blooms large and pale
3 Crawford's Early	G	M	Very large, bright yellow and red; flesh also yellow. A magnificent variety; blooms very small and pale
4 Royal George	S	M	Large, rosy red; good bearer; blooms small, dark red
5 Walburton Admirable	G	L	Very large, greenish-white; flowers small. The latest variety which ripens in all seasons in a cold-house
6 French Galande, or } Bellegarde	G	M	Large, dark red; flowers small
7 Early York	S	E	Medium size, rosy red; flowers large. The best early variety
8 Pêche Abec	G	M	Medium, rosy red, very handsome; flowers large
9 English Galande, or } Violette Hâtive	G	M	Large, dark red; flowers small
10 Early Newington	R	M	Large, rosy red, very beautiful; small flowers
11 George the Fourth	G	M	Large, light red; small flowers
12 Malta	S	M	Large, greenish-white, pink next the sun, succeeds Royal George; flowers large and very pale
13 Barrington	G	M	Large, red; flowers large
14 Acton Scott	G	E	Medium, red; flowers large
15 Early Anne	S	E	Rather small, pale green and red, very early; flowers large
16 Belle Bausse	G	L	Large, dark red, very handsome, but often inferior in flavour; flowers large

17 Reine es ergers	R	L	Very large and beautiful, rosy red, often woolly and inferior; flowers small
18 Late Admirable	G	L	Large, green and red. This, with its varieties Têton de Venus and Boudin, seldom ripen here so as to be of good quality without heat; flowers small
19 Salway	R	L	Large, pale yellow. Like the last named, wants heat to ripen with us in most seasons; flowers small
20 Red Nutmeg	R	E	Very small, pale red, a worthless curiosity; flowers large

Some new French and American varieties are omitted, as their value in the climate of the midland counties has not yet been proved. The whole of the above are melting Peaches.

NECTARINES.

1 Balgowan	R	M	Large, green and red; flowers small
2 Pitmaston Orange	G	M	Large, yellow and red; flowers very large and handsome. Rivers' Seedling Pitmaston Orange resembles this in every particular, except in having reniform in place of globose glands.
3 Violette Hâtive	R	M	Medium, red and green; flowers small; flesh much rayed with red at the stone

4 Elruge	R	M	Resembles the above; flesh white at the stone; both are excellent; flowers small
5 Hardwick Seedling	S	M	Medium size, red and green; large flowers
6 Downton	R	M	Resembles Elruge; small flowers
7 Hunt's Tawney	S	E	Small, red and yellow; good bearer; flowers small
8 Stanwick	R	L	Large, red and green, requires a good climate to ripen, and is seldom good without heat; when forced it is one of the best; flowers large
9 Neate's White	R	M	Medium, white; flowers large and pale; rather acid except in hot summers

All these are melting Nectarines. The Newington, Roman, and Early Newington are omitted, being clingstones and rarely good.

Exterior View of Orchard-house built by Mr. R. Foster, of
Beeston, for the Chilwell Nurseries.

GLASS FOR GREENHOUSES.

JAMES PHILLIPS & Co. beg to summit their prices as follows:—

ENGLISH GLASS, 16 ozs. to the foot, in Sheets averaging 40 by 30, packed in cases containing about 280 feet, 2¼d. and 2½d. per foot.

SHEET GLASS, 16 ounces, packed in boxes of 100 feet each. Package included.

				3rds.	4ths.
12 by 9	13 by 9	14 by 9	15 by 9 ⎱	14 0	12 6
12 „ 10	13 „ 10	14 „ 10	15 „ 10 ⎰		
13 „ 11	14 „ 11	15 „ 11	16 „ 11		
14 „ 12	15 „ 12	16 „ 12	17 „ 12	16 0	13 6
18 „ 12	19 „ 12	20 „ 12	16 „ 13	per 100 ft.	
17 „ 13	18 „ 13	19 „ 13	20 „ 13		
16 „ 14	17 „ 14	18 „ 14	20 „ 14		

Various other sizes.

Glass for Orchard-houses.

As supplied by us to Mr. Rivers, and the Royal Horticultural Society.

		16 ozs.		21 ozs.
		£ s. d.		£ s. d
20 in. by 12 in. ⎰				
20 in. by 13 in.	Common	0 13 6	..	0 18 0
20 in. by 14 in.	Superior	0 16 0	..	1 3 0
20 in. by 15 in. ⎱	English Glass......	0 18 0	..	1 9 0

The above prices include the Boxes.

Small Sheet Squares.

In 100 feet Boxes.

6 by 4	6½ by 4½	7 by 5	7½ by 5½ ⎱	.... 11 6
8 by 6	8½ by 6⅜	9 by 7	9½ by 7½ ⎰	
		10 by 8	10½ by 8½	...... 12 6

Boxes 2s. each, returnable at full price.

Squares Cut to Special Sizes.

16 oz.—4ths, 1¾d., 2d., and 2½d.   21 oz. 2¾d., 3d., and 3½d.
„   3rds. 2d., 2½d., and 3d.   „   3d., 2¼d., and 4d.

London Agents for Hartley's Improved Patent Rough Plate.

Linseed Oil, Genuine White Lead, Carson's Paints, Paints of various colours ground ready for use.

Milk Pans, Propagating Glasses, and every description of Glass for Horticultural purposes.

JAMES PHILLIPS & Co.

180, BISHOPSGATE STREET WITHOUT, LONDON, E.C.

J. JONES'S
HOT-WATER APPARATUS.

MONRO'S CANNON BOILER.

PRICE.

LENGTH OF BOILER.				EACH.		
20-inch Wrought Iron	.	.	.	£3	15	0
24-inch Wrought Iron	.	.	.	6	10	0
30-inch Wrought Iron	.	.	.	7	10	0
36-inch Wrought Iron	.	.	.	8	10	0
48-inch Wrought Iron	.	.	.	12	0	0
60-inch Wrought Iron	.	.	.	20	0	0
72-inch Wrought Iron	.	.	.	25	0	0

THESE Boilers are now acknowledged by all who who have used them to be the best Boilers at present invented. They are both economical in their first cost, and also in the consumption of fuel. They require but little space to fix them in, and when set the total height of brickwork need not be more than 3½ feet, consequently they can be fixed in many places where it would be impossible to set an Upright Boiler. These Boilers are now made of various sizes, suitable to heat from 300 to 3000 feet of 4-inch pipe, and are kept in stock and sold only by J. JONES, 6, Bankside, Southwark, London, S.E.

Prices for *Hot-water Pipes, Elbows, Tees, Syphons, Valves, Trough Pipes, Ornamental Coil Cases, Beck's Patent Valves, &c.; or Estimates for Hot-water Apparatus* delivered Free to any Railway Station, or erected complete in any part of the country, with *Cannon, Saddle,* or *Cylinder Boilers,* will be sent, with an *Illustrated Catalogue,* free on application.

J. JONES,
Hot-water Apparatus Manufactory, 6, Bankside, London, S.E.

www.ingramcontent.com/pod-product-compliance
Lightning Source LLC
Chambersburg PA
CBHW022038080426
42733CB00007B/888